MW01065249

CLOSE-UP
A Focus on Nature

SILVER BURDETT PRESS
© 1995 Silver Burdett Press
Published by Silver Burdett Press.
A Simon & Schuster Company
299 Jefferson Road, Parsippany, NJ 07054
Printed in the United States of America
10 9 8 7 6 5 4 3 2 1

Library of Congress
Cataloging-in-Publication Data
Holing, Dwight.
    Coral reefs/by Dwight Holing;photographs by Frank
Balthis . . . [et al.].
        p. cm. -- (Close up)
Originally published: San Luis Obispo, Calif.:
Blake Pub., ©1990.
Includes bibliographical references (p.).
    ISBN 0-382-24857-0 (LSB)
    ISBN 0-382-24858-9 (SC)
    1. Coral reef biology--Juvenile literature. 2. Coral
reefs and islands--Juvenile literature. [1. Corals. 2. Coral
reefs and islands. 3. Coral reef animals.] I. Balthis, Frank,
ill. II. Title. III. Series: Close up (Parsippany, N.J.)
QH95.8.H65   1994
574.9'1--dc20   94-30868
                                                         CIP
                                                         AC

Coral Reefs

WRITER
Dwight Holing

SERIES EDITOR
Vicki León

PHOTOGRAPHERS
Frank Balthis, Tom Bean, Dorothy Cutter,
Howard Hall, Helmut Horn, Chris Newbert, Doug Perrine,
Lindsay Pratt, Ed Robinson, Carl Roessler, Geoffrey Semorile,
Marty Snyderman, Norbert Wu

DESIGNER
Ashala Nicols-Lawler

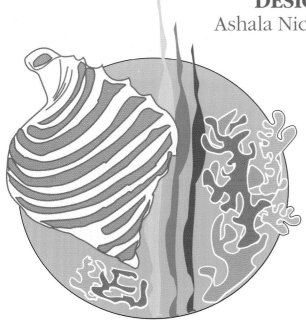

SILVER BURDETT PRESS

© 1995 Silver Burdett Press
Published by Silver Burdett Press.
A Simon & Schuster Company
299 Jefferson Road,
Parsippany, NJ 07054
Printed in the United States of America
10 9 8 7 6 5 4 3 2 1

SCHOOL COLORS. *Countless species of boldly colored fishes, such as these basslets in Fiji, flash and spin in great dizzying schools about the reef. Adding to the brilliance are soft corals, shown here in a bouquet of pinks and reds. Oddly enough, the most subdued characters on the reef are often the reef-builders themselves, the hard corals. Pictured is a tree coral, one of many reef-building species.*

FRAGILE CITIES
BENEATH THE SEA

Growing in the warm and shallow waters of the world, strange things lie barely hidden. Tiny creatures of antiquity more plant than animal build secret cities on the skeletons of their dead. Technicolor walls of living matter shield leopard spotted eels that spring like ghoulish jack-in-the-boxes. Elegantly armored crabs scuttle after leftovers dropped by sharks. Clouds of translucent, bug-eyed shrimp swirl over coral gardens. Curtains of silvery anchovies shimmer against the deepening blue. And everywhere you look, masses of fishes in Day-Glo colors and eccentric shapes spin and zigzag in a nonstop carousel of color.

■ Welcome to the coral reef – the most complex and dazzling habitat on earth, and still the most mysterious. Humans have long been drawn to coral's beauty but remained ignorant of its origins until the 1800s. It took Charles Darwin, father of the theory of evolution, to discover how and why coral reefs are formed. His quest triggered a scientific debate about the curious paradox of coral reefs. How do tropical seas which are as poor in nutrients as sand in a desert support such bountiful underwater oases? The answer, we now know, lies with the coral polyp, chief ingredient in this saltwater bouillabaisse: a simple, multicellular animal that joins forces with a plant to prosper.

■ Related to the anemone, a flowery creature that inhabits tidepools and reefs, the pinhead-sized coral polyp resembles a chrysanthemum but has an appetite like a Venus flytrap. Shiva-like tentacles called nematocysts surround a puckery mouth. The polyp uses these stinging darts to zap zooplankton, its favorite meal.

■ Not all corals build reefs. Those polyps that do put Frank Lloyd Wright to shame. Reef-building polyps

can build structures that dwarf Manhattan sky-scrapers. To survive, the soft-bodied polyp secretes a protective cup of calcium carbonate, or lime-stone, about its body. Microscopic algae living inside the polyp help produce this skeletal material. Called zooxanthellae (literally "animal-loving plant"), this hard-working helpmate takes up car-bon and phosphates dissolved in sea water and converts them into sugar and amino acids, which the polyp munches down as food. The process eases and speeds the conversion of calcium and carbon dioxide into limestone, allowing the coral reef to grow. What does the alga get out of all this? Access to sunlight, its main requirement. That's why reef-building corals need clear, shallow water – so the sun can reach them.

*T*he polyp secretes limestone throughout its life, continuously extending the length of its stony cup. And since the coral polyp abhors being a lonely guy, it connects itself to other like-minded polyps to form colonies. The cumulative effect? Thousands of generations of polyps eventually connect and lengthen their cups, making a reef composed of ancestral skeletons at the base and live polyps on the surface. Reefs are made even stronger by coralline algae, which acts as cement for the coral organisms. The largest living structures on earth, coral reefs often grow to an unbelievable size. Linked colonies can stretch for hundreds of miles. Coral currently covers 80 million square miles of the globe. If massed into a single reef, it would measure 25 times the size of the continental United States.

■ Polyps capable of forming limestone skeletons or stony corals come in many shapes and sizes. Their descriptive names say it all: brain, blind man's cane, vase, elkhorn, umbrella, mushroom, plate, medusa, and hundreds more.

■ A second type called soft corals sprouts underwater blooms as leafy as jungle plants. They grow more rapidly than their stony siblings. The immense soft corals of the Indo-Pacific, for instance, can reach six feet in height. Like stony coral, they form colonies composed of thousands of individuals. But instead of secreting limestone cups, these soft-skinned polyps form huge, inflatable bags made of secreted rubbery tissue to elevate themselves into the food

WHICH WAY IS UP? *For soft corals, found in abundance wherever reefs are present, growing up, down, or sideways is a matter of indif-ference. Their fleshy bodies, stiffened with calcium sclerites, reach enormous size and come in a range of colors to gladden a decorator's heart. Although related to hard corals, soft corals are fragile colonizers rather than reef builders.*

stream. When the currents stop, or when the sun is high and the zooxanthellae active, the colonies deflate their bags and let their algae tenants feed them.

■ Corals bloom in a mad profusion of colors, from fiery reds to soft pinks, from royal purple to burnished gold. Stony corals tend to be softer shades, such as cream, brown, or green. Soft corals explode with brilliance. Different pigments within the cells of the algae that resides in the coral polyps account for the spectrum of colors. The pigments play a major role in trapping light and in photosynthesis – the same technique plants use to turn sunlight into life-giving energy. Because light is changed by the amount of water through which it must pass, the various pigments permit coral to live in a variety of depths.

Scientists divide coral reefs into four classes. They call a reef built around a central lagoon where a volcanic mountain has collapsed an atoll. Water barely covers the top of the reef, and the lagoon often contains small islands made of coral and other sea life ground into sand. Atolls vary in size. You could build 15,000 Egyptian-style pyramids with the amount of coral contained in the average-sized atoll. The largest is Kwajalein in the Pacific Ocean. It surrounds a lagoon over 60 miles long. The most famous is Bikini. Its name synonymous with skimpy swimwear, this doughnut-shaped atoll suffered nuclear bombardment by the U.S. Army in the 1950s. Amazingly, coral polyps continue to sprout on the still-radioactive reef.

■ Barrier reefs dwarf all other types in size and grandeur. Australia's Great Barrier Reef, largest in the world, stretches over 1,200 miles and contains more sculpted and variegated landscape than the Grand Canyon. Barrier reefs are also found in the Caribbean, off Belize and in the Bahamas.

■ Most reefs fall into the fringing class. Smaller than barriers, they cling to shore. The shallow landward side typically rises out of the water while the sunken seaward side pushes toward the horizon, expanding at an astonishing rate. Patch reefs fall into the final classification. You'll spot these small, isolated coral heads sprouting out of sandy or grassy sea bottoms. Despite their small stature, patch reefs support a fantasyland of different species.

■ Don't bother looking for coral reefs outside of the narrow band of ocean that circles the globe between

DISTURBING A DELICATE BALANCE. *Fringing reefs at Palau in the South Pacific seas offer a rare side-by-side combination of tropical rainforest and coral reef habitats. Admired by divers for the splendor and clarity of its diving conditions, Palau's waters now are being muddied from silt runoff caused by logging on the islands.*

the Tropics of Cancer and Capricorn. Reef-building coral needs warm water – about 70 degrees Fahrenheit. The water must be free of sediment, sand, and slime also. That's why coral can't get a foothold off the coasts of Brazil, India, or West Africa. The mighty rivers in those regions flush too much mud into the ocean. Most corals flourish in waters shallower than 135 feet. But red, black, and other coral species can be found much deeper. Solitary corals live in deeper, cooler waters but do not build reefs.

■ Long ago coral covered most of the planet, but geological events of epic proportions limited its range and restricted the size of reefs. Coral polyps first appeared on Earth over 500 million years ago; their history is recorded in fossils buried all over the globe.

■ Early in its evolutionary history, coral inhabited a vast circumglobal body of water which connected all of the world's oceans: the Tethys Sea. Picture this singular sea as a giant aquarium. What swam on one side of the tank could also be found swimming on the other. Many, many coral species lived here.

■ All that changed some 25 million years ago. Continents drifted. Ice ages came and went. The sea rose and fell. Eventually Eurasia and Africa were connected by a land bridge. The Indo-Pacific took over as the center of coral development, while the animals on the other side of the world were largely confined to the warm, shallow waters of the Caribbean Sea. Then, 10 to 15 million years ago, the newly formed Isthmus of Panama cut Caribbean corals off altogether from their Indo-Pacific cousins.

■ Consequently, coral types and reef systems differ widely on either side of the land barrier. Though approximately 100 classes of coral exist on a worldwide basis, only eight grow in both areas. Some 60 different species of coral live in the Caribbean, compared to more than 700 in the Indo-Pacific. The number and size of reefs also varies. Barrier reefs are few; the major one runs parallel to the coast of Belize in Central America. Only ten Caribbean reefs can

Triggerfish: Not just blowing hot air

Fifteen inches of bad temper, the triggerfish sports teeth that can crack a clam shell. Jacques Cousteau says the aggressive fish's ivories can do a number on fingers, too. During a trip to the Indian Ocean, a Cousteau diver had his mitts nipped by a mother guarding her eggs.

Triggerfish have another weapon in their arsenal. They can blow powerful jets of water with firehose velocity. Usually they do so to churn up the sandy bottom, revealing small crabs and mollusks. In another variation, they blast sea urchins and knock them over. While the spiny echinoderm is up-ended, the triggerfish dashes in and makes a meal out of the unprotected underside.

Triggerfish dress in vivid blues, shiny golds, burnished browns, and bright whites and in a variety of patterns: stripes, bars, speckles, and spots. Most noticeable ornament is its defensive spine that can be raised at will and locked into place. When chased by a bigger fish, the triggerfish flees into a coral formation and uses its raised spine to anchor itself into a protected position.

9

CORAL FAMILIES. *Often recognizable by their shapes and textures, hard or stony corals predominate in the large photograph, adorned with the rubbery blue arms of a cobalt sea star and a banded sea snake. Other family members include hydrozoan coral, also called fire coral for the mean little spines on its branches. Despite its shape, it is more akin to jellyfish than to the true corals.*

be called atolls while the fringing and patch reefs here tend to be smaller than their western counterparts. On the other hand, the Indo-Pacific boasts no less than 300 atolls. You won't be disappointed by the number of barrier reefs, either. Good luck trying to count them all.

■ The greatest disparity between the two regions is measured by the number of invertebrate and vertebrate species found in each area. Take tropical fish. While no list can be complete because biologists identify new species regularly, about 500 species of fish swim around Caribbean reefs, compared to more than 3,000 species in the Indo-Pacific.

■ Despite their differences, Caribbean and Indo-Pacific coral reefs share one important quality: both support a bounty of biological riches. One-quarter or more of the world's estimated 15,000 marine algae species and 500,000 marine animal species live in, on, or around coral reefs.

The three-dimensional nature of reefs has much to do with the Noah's Ark-like conditions. Coral reefs grow every which way but loose – horizontally, diagonally, and vertically. Overhanging balconies, level stretches, gorges, terraces, caves, hollows, pedestals, and clefts make for more habitats than the Amazon. Varying degrees of sunshine, shade, water temperature, and current further divide up the turf. No wonder coral reefs win the popularity contest among marine plants and animals. There's no shortage of homes.

■ Coral reefs work much like our own big cities. Distinctive communities – underwater equivalents to a Chinatown, a Little Italy, a Spanish Harlem – house a United Nations of different species. On the surface of the reefs you have sedentary creatures like anemones, sponges, sea squirts, and barnacles. You might think these denizens rather dull. Far from it. The segmented polychaete worm, for instance, has little in common with your average nightcrawler. These little wrigglers measure about the length of your finger and conceal their bodies in tubes of sand and

S FISHES MOUTH OFF FOR MANY REASONS. *In the top picture, a parrotfish spins itself a nightly nest of mucus from its mouth. The see-through cocoon may confuse predators that hunt by smell. In the middle photo, a pair of male wrasses square off in a territorial display. Like males of many species, fishes make open-mouth gestures or puff up their bodies to beat out the competition. Besides being a place to eat, sleep, hunt, and mate, the coral reef offers cleaning stations for its inhabitants. Certain spots get designated as neutral territory. By making "I want to be cleaned" gestures, fishes line up for services performed by smaller fry without either party being preyed upon. Payment? The price of a meal, no doubt.*

mucus. When they feel hungry, they pop out of their tubular homes like a piece of rye out of the toaster and unfurl a battery of sticky appendages to snag a quick meal. The Christmas tree serpulid looks just like its name. Found on coral reefs throughout the tropical world, it extends its delicate, feathery limbs so that unsuspecting plankton and larvae stick to them like flies to a spider's web. Some yuletide dinner.

I nvertebrates such as the tiny shell-covered organisms called copepods creep around the reef's walls, creating a living motion picture. Prima ballerinas of the reef, crinoids or feather stars tend to hog the spotlight. A pair of these plumy-legged dancers will suddenly rise up on their points and perform a pas de deux, climaxing in a series of pirouettes. The seastar family is well represented, although few coral varieties are as simple and familiar as tidepool seastars. The Ophidiaster has arms a foot long. The many-armed Heliaster off the Galapagos Islands looks like an underwater hedgehog.

■ Lobsters, crabs, and shrimp lurk in nooks and crannies, bored into the substrate by bivalves that leave the reef as holey as Swiss cheese. Mimicking stony coral, these members of the Arthropoda family produce external skeletons of shell that protect their bodies against injury. Despite their imposing armor, these clanging underwater knights are nothing more than scavengers who skulk along the bottom in search of leftovers. Unlike the standard Maine variety, coral lobsters display a palette of colors that would do Picasso proud. The painted lobster's shell is splashed like an abstract canvas. You'd hardly recognize the slipper lobster as a shellfish at all. Its flattened body and flared skirt are more reminiscent of an inverted clawfoot bathtub. Crabs and shrimp also display exotic markings. One species of cleaner shrimp has candy-cane stripes just like a barber pole. You won't find the decorator crab going anywhere without its parasol – a living umbrella made of sponges that it holds over its back with a pair of contortionist's legs.

■ Some of the creepiest creatures slipping in and out of coral reefs have neither feet nor fin. Slithery and silent, sea snakes descend from the surface to the seafloor to stalk their prey. They can hold their breath for up to two hours. Moray eels reign as the kings of the crevices.

DAY SHIFT, NIGHT SHIFT. *Reefs sometimes form circular lagoons or blue holes. This photo was taken in Belize. Other blue holes are found in the Bahamas and around Australia. Topside and underwater offer contrasting views of the reef. So do day and night. Because many hard corals only extend their polyps to feed at night, their daytime aspect can be very different. At far left you see the pink branches of Acropora, one of the world's commonest and most varied hard corals.*

CALLING ALL CRINOIDS.

Tousle-headed crinoids, more prettily called feather stars, bring color, form, and drama to the reef. An echinoderm like the sea star and the sea cucumber, crinoids wave their feathery arms about to collect minute bits of food. With five to 200 arms per crinoid, they do pretty well. At night, feather stars crawl or swim to a favored filtering position. Once there, they appear to stand on tiptoe, balanced on their cirri or grasping organs and swaying gently in the current. Often found on vertical reef walls, crinoids typically position themselves on contrasting colors of algae or sponges, much to the delight of underwater photographers.

EQUAL PARTNERS. *Everywhere you look on the coral reef, creatures cooperate to survive. When both parties benefit, it's called symbiosis. Here, a blenny fish hides in brain coral, its hole probably made by a boring clam. The green of the brain coral comes from zooxanthellae, algal plants living inside its tissues. The algae gains a good home in sunlit waters so it can make its own food. The coral gets nutrients from the algae, plus the ability to build its reef faster.*

The giant moray stretches the tape at six feet or more. Some morays behave as ferociously as they look. The viper moray, for instance, uses its curved six-inch long jaws to snatch passing fish or pluck crustaceans from their hide-outs. Garden eels prefer the sandy bottom; a colony of their eerily waving bodies is a sight to behold.

■ Shelless snails, also known as nudibranchs, share this neck of the reef. These tiny predators sport more color combinations than a spring fashion catalog. The Spanish dancer nudibranch, for instance. It may not move with flamenco rhythm, but it has all the grace and just as gaudy a costume. Browsing among the corals and the sponges like carnivorous cows in a meadow, they chug across the reef in one

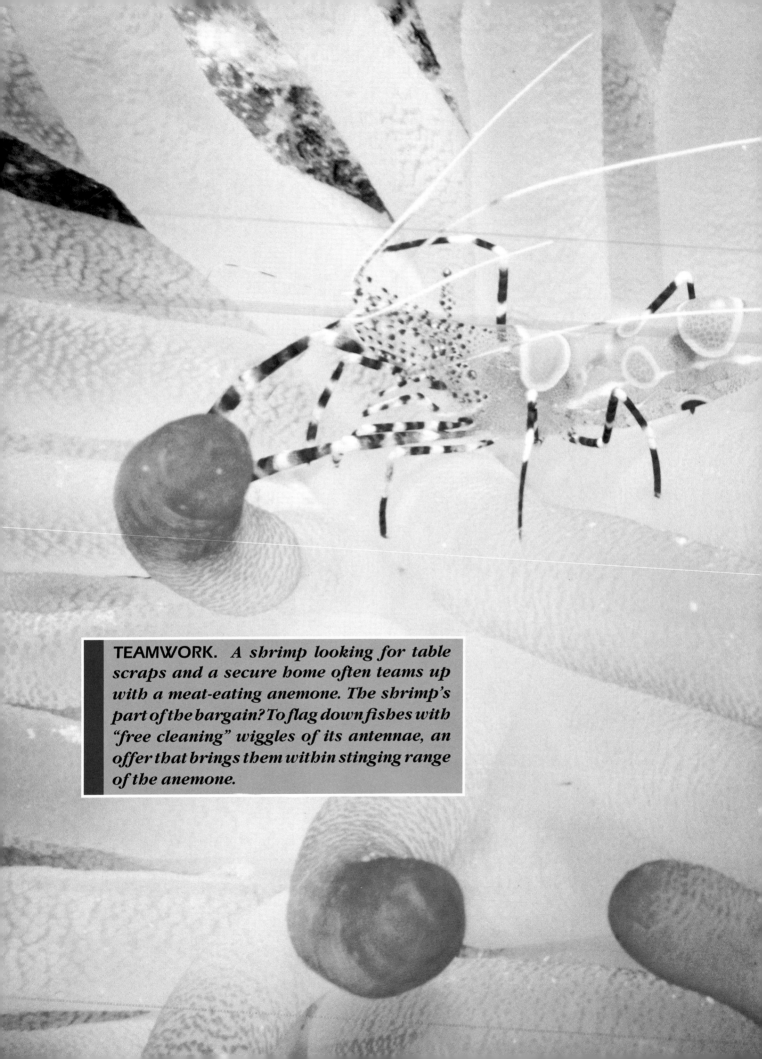

TEAMWORK. *A shrimp looking for table scraps and a secure home often teams up with a meat-eating anemone. The shrimp's part of the bargain? To flag down fishes with "free cleaning" wiggles of its antennae, an offer that brings them within stinging range of the anemone.*

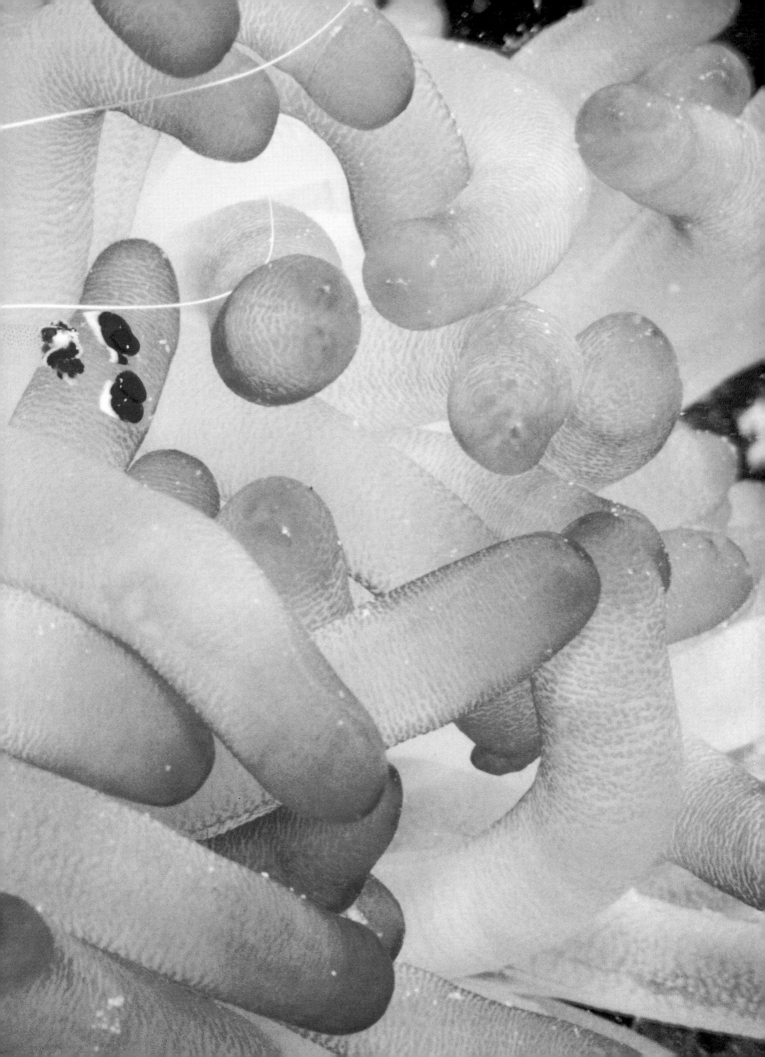

unhurried meal. Hand-like underbellies allow them to stick to any surface.

■ When it comes to being the most eye-catching, reef fish take the prize. Consider this: for every tropical fish you've seen circling in an aquarium or on a public television special, a hundred other types swim beneath the surface of the sea. Coral reef fishes come in more vibrant colors than the neon lights along the Las Vegas strip. They also display a greater variety of behavior than you'll see acted out on Broadway. Surgeonfish look like pancakes smeared with butter and dripping with blueberries. The black and yellow butterflyfish has a snout that would give Jimmy Durante pause. The prodigious proboscis lets it graze on coral without stinging its eyes. Parrotfish not only glow green and blue like their feathered namesakes, they also sport powerful chisel-toothed beaks which enable them to crunch coral, spewing it out as sand. A single parrotfish produces five tons of sand a year. When you see masses of fluorescent angelfishes or fairy basslets dart and flicker in sparkling tropical water, you'd think you were watching a psychedelic light show at a rock concert.

■ Coral reefs have an almost urban quality to them. Space is at a premium, resources limited, violence commonplace. Every inhabitant has an enemy. Eat or be eaten makes a simple but unforgiving rule to live by. The fact that most species must share a dinner table with those that view them as the main course further complicates the situation. To survive, coral reef species rely on wondrous defense mechanisms, feeding behaviors, and mating rituals.

MOONSTRUCK. *Like a slow-motion snowstorm in reverse, coral colonies spawn en masse. Rarely photographed but known to occur one or two nights a year on the Great Barrier Reef, coral spawning is governed by lunar cycles. What makes these tiny creatures stake their reproductive chances on a one-night stand? Perhaps because they are able to hedge their bets by reproducing themselves asexually as well.*

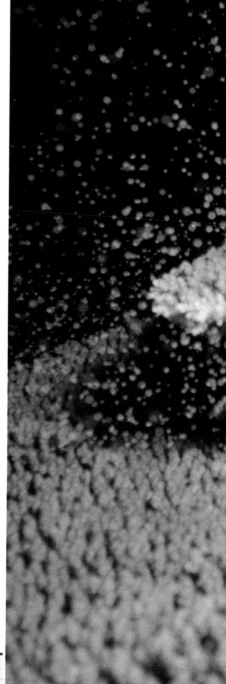

24

Take schooling, for instance. Dozens, hundreds, even thousands of fish swim about the reefs in unison. Fishes school for speed. Just as bicycle riders can take advantage of reduced wind resistance by pedaling behind a car, fish benefit from reduced water resistance. Fish also school to avoid predators. The old theory of safety in numbers has never rung more true. When a predator strikes, it is distracted by the movement of all the swimmers. Schooling also means more lookouts, making it harder for the enemy to launch a sneak attack. Fish move as one in order to search for food more effectively and to muscle in on someone else's territory. Check out the convict surgeonfish. These striped bullies team up to invade algae fields defended by lavender tangs. Schooling allows species to maintain their identity. It also makes finding a mate a whole lot easier.

Fish form colonies primarily for reproductive reasons. Clown wrasses live in harems; so do whitetailed humbugs. Other fish pick a mate and live as happily married couples. A pair of butterflyfish bond so tightly that one member will stop feeding and go look for its mate if they become separated. When they reunite, they celebrate with a little ritual – swimming around each each other at close range for a few minutes.

Most fish stake claims to a particular part of the reef. Territory provides them with a ready source of food

BITE-SIZED BEAUTIES. *On the reef, even tiny flatworms and bristleworms wear spectacular costumes. These carnivores often hunt on gorgonian, a willowy, non-building coral that can live on reefs and in temperate waters alike. Like sea slugs or nudibranchs, the vivid colors of the worms often serve to advertise their inedibility. One bitter or stinging mouthful, and would-be predators learn to leave these noxious rainbows alone.*

and shelter. Some fish become so attached to their ancestral digs that you can take them away, release them, and they'll zoom back like homing pigeons. A scientist tried that with mottled blennies off the coast of northeast New Zealand and discovered they could find their way back six times out of ten from 700 yards away. These coral reef home boys defend their turf, too. The tiny damselfish will blitz a trespasser no matter what their size. The blueline surgeonfish patrols its territory by swimming in patterns around its boundaries. When other fish come close, the blueline swims parallel to the intruder in an attempt to herd it away.

Despite so much territoriality, tight living quarters spurs some coral citizens into forming alliances with neighbors who would otherwise be sworn enemies. You see symbiotic relationships throughout the animal kingdom, but you'll never find as many odd couples as you do on tropical reefs. The clownfish and anemone take the cake as the strangest bedfellows. Most fish avoid anemones like the plague because of their stinging tentacles, but the clownfish embraces these weapons with all the ardor of a lover. It spends its life swimming in and out of the tentacles, even nesting among them. To keep from getting stung, the clownfish wears a mucous coat and the anemone fails to recognize it as food. What does the anemone get out of this arrangement? No one is certain, but biologists suspect that the clownfish provides a cleaning service, picking up table scraps dropped by the messy feeder.

■ The long-spined sea urchin also wins a good neighbor award. In East Indian waters, for example, urchins shelter shrimpfish and clingfish that wiggle in and out of the guardian needles. The mismatched sponge and shrimp are symbiotic partners. Wring out a single loggerhead sponge from the West Indies and out fall 16,000 shrimp.

■ These symbiotic relationships mean life on a coral reef isn't all big fish eating little fish. With a single gulp, the enormous grouper could make quite a snack out of a hundred tiny gobies, but it never would. Instead, the big lunk opens its cavernous mouth and allows the tiny fingerlings inside to perform their own brand of dental hygiene. Other living-together arrangements on the reef

SNUG HARBOR. *Simple and soft sponges may be the reef's most ancient animals. Their porous bodies often host hundreds of fishes, shrimps, and others. Found worldwide, sponge growths and colors are especially magnificent around the Caribbean.*

Sponges: Not a plant but an animal, honest

Take a sponge, tear it into pieces, pass it through a sieve and what do you get? A lot of little sponges. These incredibly soft and, well, spongy masses are actually primitive multicellular animals that have been kicking around the world for more than 600 million years. As the photo shows, they often spawn by releasing clouds of sperm and eggs into the water.

Made from several different minerals, sponges consist mostly of chambers which allow large volumes of water to be pumped through their bodies. Purpose? To extract bits of floating food, mainly plankton. The animals themselves have about as much nutritional value as sponge cake. That doesn't stop puffer fish and cowries from treating them like dessert, however.

Shrimp, fish, and crabs find shelter in the creature's por-ous body. Some barrel sponges in Caribbean waters get so big that two divers can squat inside of one.

include commensalism, where one party benefits and the other remains unaffected. Sharks, for example, let remoras, eel-shaped fish with mouths like Hoover vacuum cleaners, hitchhike on their bodies.

■ Not all reef creatures great and small coexist peacefully. There remains the pursuit of breakfast, lunch, and dinner. Most coralfish dine at dawn and dusk – scientists call this time of day "crepuscular." If you want to see fish at their most active, plan your dives or trips to the aquarium accordingly.

■ Some fish graze, others farm. Most hunt. Angelfish, trunkfish, and triggerfish cruise over the coral surface munching on mollusks, algae, and worms. Butterflyfish belong to the Chaetodontidae family – Greek for "bristle tooth." Their fine, hairlike teeth make short work of tubeworms and sponges. Wrasses have snake-like hinged jaws. They open wide for all sizes of crabs and snails. Rear molars crush the thick shells as easily as a nutcracker shatters walnuts. Combtoothed and sabretoothed blennies have teeth like, well, you get the picture.

■ Threespot damselfish are coral reef farmers. These saltwater sodbusters cultivate algae on tiny plots the size of a paperback. While they never have to worry about droughts or grain embargos, they do have to contend with sea urchins that, if given the chance, will mow down an algae field like a combine cutting wheat. Marine biologists at the Discovery Bay Marine Laboratory in Jamaica have studied how Caribbean threespots deal with these spiny intruders. Clearly, offense is the best defense. Threespots charge in as fearlessly as the Light Brigade, biting the urchin where it counts. If they can't drive an urchin off, they'll carry it off. The plucky threespot grabs hold of a short spine with its teeth, picks the urchin up, and hauls it away, dumping it unceremoniously on someone else's turf.

■ Hunting season remains open all year long on coral reefs. That's why you'll find camouflage dress always in style. Hunter and hunted alike depend on coloring and the ability to change it for survival. Quick-change artists like flounder melt into the background by mimicking whatever surface they

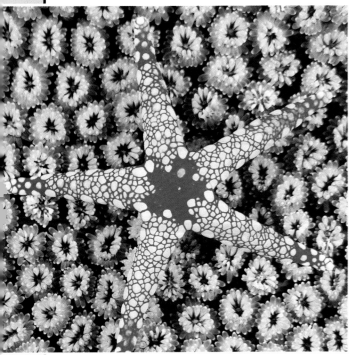

glide over. In one laboratory experiment, a flounder was actually able to match the pattern of a checkerboard. Not only does the octopus constantly change colors, it can also alter its skin texture at will.

■ Most fish have either bars or stripes. The vertical and horizontal markings help conceal their presence. The redband yellowtail turns pale and develops two black stripes the length of its body when it hides in a forest of sea whips. Bar patterns disrupt a fish's body outline, making them a more confusing target when pursued. False eyespots on the foureye butterfly fish fluster predators as well. Which pair do you zero in on?

■ Predators rely on camouflage for the element of surprise, the key to successful ambush. Take a closer look next time you spot a colony of sponges. The one with the grim, steady eyes is actually a frogfish, a chameleonlike creature that can change its color as well as its spots to blend in with its varied neighborhood. The frogfish has another trick up its scaly sleeve. Attached to its nose is a fleshy wattle shaped like a fishing pole. And that's exactly how the frogfish uses it. While lying motionless on the bottom, the piscine angler will bob the built-in lure to tempt curious fish. Few can resist the bait. When they strike, the frogfish opens its massive maw and the would-be diner becomes dinner.

■ The trumpetfish plays a different tune, but one just as deadly. A relative of the seahorse, these tube-shaped predators make like branches by hanging from sea fans or treelike gorgonian coral. As soon as an unwary fish passes by, bingo! Breakfast. For its next number, the trumpetfish straddles a passing parrotfish, for example, and uses it for cover. This allows it to get closer to unsuspecting victims.

■ Food isn't the only thing coral reef species have a healthy appetite for. There's also sex. A lot of sex. Most species reproduce prolifically to keep themselves from being eaten out of house and home and into extinction. Much of the mating is done to the light of the moon. Though scientists don't know exactly how the moon influences reproductive behavior, they suspect tidal fluctuations have something to do with it. The moon's light may be as important as its gravitational pull. Some fish use moonlight so they can guard their nests around

WILLING TO PAY AN ARM AND A LEG.

Constellations of seastars cover reefs from the Virgin Islands, right, to Hawaii with gaudy colors and patterns. Like their more subdued cousins in cooler waters, coral seastars hunt meat on the hoof and are themselves hunted. Their main getaway tactic? Shed a limb for the hunter to dine on. In an adaptation called autotomy, seastars then grow new arms at leisure.

Montastrea annularis: Star of the coral world

Montastrea annularis – don't be put off by the high-faluting name, just call it "star" – outshines most other corals when it comes to building reefs and harboring different species. The pint-sized polyp grows at a rate of ten millimeters in diameter a year – that's the coral equivalent of running a 4-minute mile.

Polyps bud in round cups, and colonies usually take the shape of massive boulders. If space is tight, however, the star will sprout branches just like a tree. An aggressive species, it attacks other corals in order to claim more space for itself. When the star detects a target, it opens up a hole in its own body and sends out a jet of digestive juice that eats away the enemy.

The star coral has universal appeal. An important builder in the Atlantic, it is one of the few corals that also grows in the Indo-Pacific.

the clock. The black clownfish breeds on a strict lunar schedule. Females lay anywhere from 200 to 400 eggs twice a month. The hatchlings emerge either during the full or new moon when reef waters are at their highest and swiftest. The full tides carry with them an abundance of planktonic larvae, easy pickings for the newborns.

■ Reef dwellers have sex in pairs and en masse. The monogamous goby, for instance, mates for life. A pair will excavate an elaborate burrow on the sea bottom where the female lays her eggs. She exits shortly after so the male can take over. To make sure he does his job, the female seals him inside the nest for three to four days. Finally she lets her spouse out so they can tend the nest together.

■ Bluehead wrasse, lyre-tail coralfish, and some hamlets lean towards group sex. You'll know it's orgy time when you see entire colonies behaving as if they were plugged into an electric eel. The swimmers begin quivering, undulating, and darting about in exaggerated U-shaped patterns. When a pack reaches the top of the U, the supermales pick a ripe female and in one long, gyrating rush, mix sperm and eggs. Supermales waste no time basking in the afterglow. As soon as they finish with one partner, it's on to the next. Caribbean sponges do it all together and all at once. In late August, entire communities of male and female sponges engage in one great orgasm. The collective release of sperm and eggs looks like billowy clouds floating through the water. Locals refer to this phenomenon as "smoking sponges." Corals, too, can spawn simultaneously. On the Great Barrier Reef, 128 species of coral fire their reproductive hopes at the same time — all within a 2-hour span, once a year!

■ Too bad Freud wasn't a marine biologist. He would have had a field day. Love among the reefs adds a whole new dimension to boy meets girl. Just as often it's boy meets boy, so one of the boys obligingly turns into a girl.

Hermaphroditism – the ability to change sexes – runs rampant on the reef. The Caribbean harlequin bass has mature reproductive organs of both sexes and can reverse its sexual functions at will, performing either as a male or a female, depending on who it meets. The wrasse, on the other hand, starts out as one sex and changes into the other. The ability to swap sex roles eliminates any problem of finding the right mate.

Changing sex also means changing wardrobes. Newly sexed fish adopt the appropriate markings to signal to potential suitors that Dick is now Jane. Color and patterns also help fish separate the men from the boys. It's not hard to pick out the supermales; the big guys outshine everybody else. Parrotfish change color three times in their lives, depending on their maturity. Color is not only used to attract members of the opposite sex, but also to discourage rivals.

■ You'd think with all that reproduction going on, coral reefs and their inhabitants would be in no danger of becoming extinct. Think again. Coral reefs have plenty of enemies, some natural, most man-made. Hurricanes and typhoons sweep through warm water shallows with the same results as Sherman's March through Georgia in the Civil War. Storms can leave toppled coral and bruised and battered fish in their wake. Too much rain can reduce a reef's salinity. A change in currents can smother coral in mud. Recovery can take years, decades, even longer. After Hurricane Hattie battered the barrier reef off Belize in 1961, scientists estimated that it would take 60 to 100 years before all was put right.

■ A greater threat comes from the crown-of-thorns seastar. This many-armed marauder has an insatiable craving for coral. A single crown-of-thorns devours about two square feet of polyps a day. A population explosion of these hungry predators has left hundreds of miles of the Great Barrier Reef stripped bare.

■ A few marine biologists blame shell collectors for decimating the triton trumpet population – a medium-sized mollusk that feeds on the rapacious seastar – thus permitting the number of crown-of-thorns to increase to their current high levels. Others believe

TROUBLE IN PARADISE. *At first glance, coral reefs from Bali to Grand Cayman appear rich, beautiful, and untroubled. Under that warm water, however, a variety of enemies threaten reef survival. To answer the demand for tropical aquarium fish, for example, gatherers use sodium cyanide to stun fish, often stunning reefs to death with repeated doses.*

that damage from this species and other natural forces is cyclical.

■ As we're now realizing, it's the activities of man that most imperil the reefs. In the Caribbean, reefs are seriously damaged by boat anchors, fishing lines, plastic debris, and siltation from construction too near the sea. In the Indo-Pacific, fishing with dynamite or cyanide kills coral reefs. So does pulverizing reef formations to make new harbors. Chopping down tropical rainforests fills waters with silt – a leading cause of reef damage in the Philippines. Equally deadly is the growing human thirst for collecting tropical fishes, coral, exotic shells, and exotic seafoods – made worse by highly destructive collecting methods.

■ By turning the ocean into a dumping ground for civilization's wastes, we're also threatening coral reefs. Spilled oil suffocates coral polyps in a toxic batter of death. Sewage contaminates shellfish. And chemical wastes poison the filter feeders. The effects of ocean pollution can be felt all the way up the food chain.

The animals of the coral world are not like other animals. They cannot flee to deeper seas that are, as yet, safe from man. The glossy cowry shell, the gorgeous sea fan, the elegant Moorish idol fish – all must live or die among the coral. It is up to us to make sure they get a fair chance. Coral reefs, among the most ancient of nature's accomplishments, have been successful because they are resilient. But even the most resilient ecosystem has its limits under the stress of human development.

■ What do the coral reefs of the world need to survive and thrive? Less tinkering with the environmentally wise ways long practiced by oceanic peoples. More respectful human development in areas where coral reefs grow. Gentler tourism. Fewer shells and coral gathering dust on the mantlepiece, more shells and coral left on the reef. Go ahead, capture the reef's beauty on film. Enjoy it in books, films, or with your own eyes. But let its splendor be.

WHAT MAKES A CORAL REEF HEALTHY? *Most agree that the fate of almost everything on the reef is tied to everything else. There are good guys like Tridacna clams, whose fleshy mantles are full of colorful algae which the clams farm. And there are bad guys like coral-crunching crown-of-thorns sea stars. But all of them –from the smallest polyp to the largest shark – are somehow important to the yin-yang balance and complexity of the coral reef.*

UNITED STATES

TEXAS

BERMUDA

BAJA

FLORIDA KEYS

HAWAIIAN ISLANDS

MEXICO

BAHAMAS

BELIZE

VIRGIN ISLANDS

GRAND CAYMAN

PANAMA

AFRICA

PACIFIC OCEAN

EQUATOR

GALAPAGOS ISLANDS

SOUTH AMERICA

ATLANTIC OCEAN

FRENCH POLYNESIA

TAHITI

Credits & Special Thanks

■ Author **Dwight Holing** has an abiding interest in natural history topics. His book credits include *California Wild Lands* and magazine work from *Audubon* to *Omni*.

■ Very special thanks for their help on this book go to: marine biologist **Jay Carroll** and Tenera Environmental; **Robert "Troutman" Allen**; **Howard Hall**; and **Helmut Horn**.

■ From the rainbow-vivid cover photo of Red Sea reefs by Chris Newbert to Helmut Horn's rare coral spawning shots on pages 22-23, this book is blessed with unusual imagery from 14 world-class photographers.

Frank Balthis: pages 34-35
Tom Bean/DRK Photo: large photo page 31

Jay Carroll: page 14, both insets
Dorothy Cutter: page 4, 11, bottom photo on 17
Howard Hall: pages 10-11, 16, top photo on 17, small photo on 31, inset on 34, large photo on 37, 40
Helmut Horn: inside front cover, page 5, 22, 22-23
Chris Newbert: front cover
Doug Perrine/DRK Photo: page 28
Lindsay Pratt: page 8, top photo on 24, 26, 32
Ed Robinson/Hawaiian Watercolors: inset on back cover; pages 2-3, bottom photo on 24, 30
Carl Roessler: pages 6-7, 26-27, 36, inset on 37
Geoffrey Semorile: back cover photo of Truk Lagoon, inside back cover, page 9, 33
Marty Snyderman: page 13 all photos, large photo on pages 14-15, 25
Norbert Wu: pages 18-19, 20-21

BOOKS & FILMS

■ Best magazine coverage: *Ocean Realm, Natural History, Sea Frontiers* Films: *Sea Fans* underwater video magazine; *The Coral Triangle*, a public television film about the problems faced by Indo-Pacific coral reefs.
Coral Kingdoms, Carl Roessler, Abrams 1986.
Underwater Guide to Hawaii, Ann Fielding and Ed Robinson, University of Hawaii Press 1987.
Howard Hall's Guide to Successful Underwater Photography, Howard Hall, Marcor Publishing 1981.
Field Guide to Caribbean Reef Invertebrates, Nancy Sefton and Dr. Stephen Webster, Sea Challengers 1986.
Reader's Digest Book of the Great Barrier Reef, R.D. Sidney, Mead & Beckett Publishing 1987.
Watching Fishes: Life and Behavior on Coral Reefs, Roberta and James Wilson, Harper & Row 1985.

38

CORAL
REEFS
WORLDWIDE

WHERE TO SEE REEFS

■ Many aquaria, marine centers, and parks offer coral reef displays and exhibits. Some are listed below, along with a partial list of living coral reefs.

■ **California**
Scripps Aquarium, La Jolla; Steinhart Aquarium, San Francisco; Sea World, San Diego; Marine World/Africa USA, Vallejo.

■ **Florida**
Pennekamp Coral Reef State Park, Biscayne National Park, Looe Key and Key Largo National Marine Sanctuaries. EPCOT Center, Disney World; Ocean World, Ft. Lauderdale; Theater of the Sea, Islamorada; Key West Aquarium; Marineland of Florida; Shipwreck Aquarium, Hialeah Park; Miami Seaquarium; Sea World of Florida in Orlando.

■ **Hawaii**
Hanauma Bay, Oahu; Molokini Cra-ter, Olowalu, Honolua Bay, and Ahihi Bay, Maui; Poipu Beach Park, Kauai; City of Refuge and Kealakekua Bay, Hawaii. Waikiki Aquarium and Sea Life Park, Oahu.

■ **Elsewhere in the U.S.**
New England Aquarium, Boston; Sea World in Aurora, Ohio; Aquarium at Niagara Falls, New York; Shedd Aquarium, Chicago; New York Aquarium, Brooklyn; National Aquarium, Baltimore; Seattle Aquarium; Mystic Marinelife Aquarium, Connecticut; Sea World of Texas.

■ **The Caribbean**
U.S. Virgin Islands, including Coral World observatory in St. Thomas and Buck Island Reef off St. Croix; Coral World Marine Park, Nassau, the Bahamas; Dutch West Antilles, especially Bonaire, the Antilles Underwater Park, and the Aquarium in Curaçao; IMB Aquarium, Lejas, Puerto Rico; Bequia, Grenadine Islands; Cayman Islands, especially Grand Cayman; Folkstone Marine Reserve, Barbados; the Bahamas, especially Andros Island.

■ **Canada & Mexico**
Vancouver Aquarium; Montreal Aquarium; Quebec Aquarium; Cabo Frailes near Cabo San Lucas, Baja California; Isla Mujeres, Cancún, and Cozumel off the Yucatán peninsula.

■ **Central & South America**
Galápagos Islands; Panamá; the barrier reef at Belize; Honduras.

■ **Europe**
Parque Oceanique Cousteau, Paris.

■ **Australia & South Pacific**
The Great Barrier Reef of Australia; Fiji Islands; Micronesia, especially Palau and Truk; Solomon Islands; Tahiti and French Polynesia; New Guinea; Philippine Islands; Indonesia; the Marianas.

■ **Indian Ocean & the Red Sea**
Seychelle Islands; Maldive Islands; Red Sea and Gulf of Aqaba at Eilat, Israel.

*There is
a natural human longing
to touch that which
is wondrous.
Love the reef but go lightly here,
so that the coral kingdom
and all its wild citizens may prosper.*

Call or write for other books in our growing nature series:

Habitats:

Tidepools ❖ *The Kelp Forest* ❖ *Icebergs & Glaciers*
Tropical Rainforests ❖ *Coral Reefs*

Marine Life:

A Raft of Sea Otters ❖ *Seals & Sea Lions*
A Pod of Gray Whales ❖ *A Pod of Killer Whales*
Humpback Whales ❖ *Sharks*

Bird Life:

Hawks, Owls & Other Birds of Prey
Parrots, Macaws & Cockatoos
A Dazzle of Hummingbirds

SILVER BURDETT PRESS

© 1995 Silver Burdett Press
Published by Silver Burdett Press.
A Simon & Schuster Company
299 Jefferson Road,
Parsippany, NJ 07054
Printed in the United States of America
10 9 8 7 6 5 4 3 2 1